MW00944163

The Truth As I Know It.(The Females guide inside the mind of the average man.)

Walter The Author

ISBN:1718962983
ISBN-13:9781718962989

DEDICATION

First I would like to thank God for given me the greatest gift that I could ever ask for and that is the ability to understand myself, others, and to be able to communicate those thoughts effectively. I would also like to thank my family and friends that encouraged and believed in me. Lastly I would like to thank the various women who have came into my life for a reason, season, or a lifetime.

FEMALES GUIDE INSIDE THE MIND OF THE AVERAGE MAN

CONTENTS

REAL MAN

Men were made to be strong, competent leaders, but the concept of a man has been forgotten in today's society. Society no longer respects the real man and most often women do not understand us either. The problem occurs because the way men and women think and do things are different. Which doesn't mean that we will not come up with the same conclusion, but our thought process to get to the final answer is almost always different. The physical, but more importantly, the mental differences between men and woman are what make the union work. Those differences should not be looked upon negatively but

1

should be celebrated because men and women are unique in there on way.

Men and woman should have defined roles in the relationship as well as the household. Woman generally run the household better because they typically multitask better. We should note the fact that we are equal but different and that those differences is what makes the human male and female relationship so dynamic. Equality, among men and women, was the general idea that was intended to bring men and women closer together in terms of work load and respect. Which in some aspects it has, but in other ways, we have over qualified the men and woman's role so much that there are no longer clearly defined lines in terms of men and woman's roles in relationships but shades of grey in which neither, the men or woman, truly knows their role in the relationships.

Women tend to be spontaneous, comprehensive thinkers meaning that woman have a better tendency to think on the fly. Women understand and consider the whole problem. They take the big picture perspective, and they view task as interconnected and interdependent. Women tend to become overwhelmed with complexities that may or may not exist and may have difficulty separating their personal experience from problems.

Men tend to focus on one problem at a time or a limited number of problems at one time. Men have an advanced ability to separate themselves from problems and minimize the different factors that may exist. Men tend to understand problems and are able to deal with the issue regardless of our emotions towards the subject. Men view problems as less interconnected and more independent. Men are likely to minimize and fail to appreciate details that can be essential to successful solutions to issues. A man may work through a problem repeatedly, talking about the same things over and over, rather than trying to address the problem as a whole.

Mentally the problems occur when we assume that

men/ women think, act, and feel the same way we do about the same situation. It's not that men and women live different realities it's just that a man's reality is not the same as a woman's and although we may share similar experiences, our perception and reactions are going to be different. The goal should always be to try and eliminate misunderstandings and communication break downs. Communication is always the key and that involves being able to talk but most importantly listen and understand those differences that make us different.

KEEPING IT REAL

Society has attempted to down grade the characteristics of a REAL man with watered down cartoon versions of how a man is and isn't supposed to act. If you look at the way men are portrayed in movies, TV, and in song lyrics, you would assume that we are highly sexual, promiscuous, and unintelligent and incapable of functioning properly without the help of a strong, intelligent woman leading the way and keeping their men in line despite his short comings. A man having a quality woman is definitely not a disadvantage but men are perfectly capable of sustaining a healthy productive life as a bachelor as well. Society makes it seem as if a man can only have success if he has a woman that is mentally superior to him "leading the way."

The media gives women the view of manliness characterized by Homer Simpson, Doug Heffernan and Martin as the typical behavior of the average man. Analyzing today's society, men are taught to look out for themselves, obtain as many material possessions as possible and be emotionally unavailable. Our society celebrates womanizing rather than applauding a man who loves one woman for a lifetime and raises a caring family and sticks with his family through the good and the bad times.

The modern musicians often sing about adulteress, promiscuous, and irresponsible behaviors and how glorious the lifestyle is. This causes some men to look up to and sub-consciously emulate the latest bad behavior that is being glorified through the various streams of media that are currently being used to promote this type of behavior.

The love for false reality and the flare for the dramatic by society have caused a lot of good men to go numb to the definition of a good man, because of the clichés like "nice guys finish last," and "good girls like bad boys". Being bad is now defined as cool and most men want to be considered cool because cool equal's bad boy and that equals a bigger variety of the type of women that are attracted to him.

Now I'm not saying that I don't fantasize about having a big booty hoe like 2chainz for my birthday or having a boo thang like Trey Songz but I also understand that as entertainers their job is to entertain it's not real and something that it used to sell records and entertain peoples fantasy's. No one should ever get to the point to where they stop being themselves in the name of popularity or for the sake of current trends in today's society. At the end of the day right is right and wrong is wrong. For every one person that realizes that it is entertainment you have three people that are living and going for broke behind the latest and current trend. Most people do it without even realizing that they are doing it and other are groupies to lifestyles that only a few are actually able to obtain, many pretend, but only a few or real and actually live that miserable life that is glorified. Real is not a word but a lifestyle and until you find your real you will never be happy with yourself or find fulfillment within yourself.

MEN OR NOT AS DUMB AS YOU THINK

Many women believe that men are dumb and can easily be lead astray due to the (sitcoms and movies which was previously discussed) and are not responsible for their actions because men are dumb, naïve, creatures' incapable of making the important decisions because we are always thinking with the wrong head. Some women feel more confident and comfortable if they are needed versus being wanted or loved. Whether she has encouraged a man's dependency on her emotionally, physically or financially as an adult, feeling needed has bolstered her self-esteem, but it has also eased abandonment concerns, which is the real basis for women that choose to make dependency based choices. At some point, most of us have heard a woman at some point say, "I don't know what he would do without me" which I personally never understood because I'm pretty sure the man wasn't found under a bridge homeless with nowhere to go before she met him. She might fear that if she lets herself love somebody as intensely as she wants to, that man will abandon her. Her sense of need feels massive, and often painful. She believes that someone on the receiving end won't be able to handle her which produces shame for being "needy." This shame makes her want to shut down her needs (or control them), which is a defense mechanism that has her giving to others, what she desperately requires for herself. It also makes her choose emotionally unavailable partners who bring back painful feelings that reinforce childhood abandonment issues. That causes her to surround herself with people that she feels needs her which in turn causes co-dependent logic which results in excessive dependency and the taking on of someone else's responsibilities and emotional well-being. What she gives to other is oftentimes what she desires to have herself.

You cannot change a person's character or behavior, only that person can change that and work through past issues and insecurities in there on life. Holding a man down maybe holding them back from fulfilling his ultimate destiny and enabling them from ever reaching their full potential. Most often the women that complain about the dead-beat men in their life oftentimes became very insecure when they surrounded themselves around people that did not have a co-dependent mentality. A man that has his own and doesn't need them frightens some people. Some that (think) they are secure in themselves sometimes take on woman with emotional and physiological baggage because of the understanding that things happen and people act out and handle situations wrong sometimes. But you must understand that when a man takes on extra baggage it's not because he's soft or weak. It's because he believes and sees potential that a woman may are may not see in herself and this also applies to women that do the same thing for men. If you find a person that is willing to accept you, with the unwritten understanding that we are all work in progress and that progression and not regression should be the number one goal. People should always be willing to make themselves better so that they can ultimately love those around them better. It's about building and growing as one. But like everything else in life everything is not meant for everybody. Oftentimes a man will leave a relationship with a co-dependent woman emotionally battered because so much was taken out of him emotionally, financially and sometimes physically so much so that when a good woman comes along he is unequipped to handle the situation.

Some woman can't handle a real man and some man

can't handle a real woman because real is hard work. The biggest choice is deciding what's real for you. Different people have different emotional and physical needs in order to feel satisfied in the relationship. There is no blue print for relationships and no such thing as perfect you simply have to find what works best for you and understand that nothing will ever be perfect. But yet we should always be striving for perfection.

4 DON'T LOVE, LOVE

Many woman claim they don't love, love but often find temporary love in a lot of different men (hoe) to keep from giving their all to that one man and to protect her heart and feelings. Sure, there will always be the cool guy, fun guy, funny guy and a whole lot of other qualities that women might find attractive in men. But should it really be hard to find all of that in one man? Sure it may require some time and a lot of effort but it is possible. But when you allow yourself to compromise and settle with good enough and even worse, having a man just to say that you have a man you end up having a void in your heart and life. The man you're dealing with may be a good guy but you may find yourself unsatisfied and unfulfilled because the man that you choose is unable to fully fulfill you because he was never what you really wanted in the first place and settled for good enough. So instead of taking the easy road and dealing with good enough, it would be better if you waited for what you really wanted, which would ultimately create less baggage that you have to carry around emotionally and less mileage you have to carry around physically, unless what you really want is a unhealthy relationship that could cause some detriment to you as an individual whether that be spiritual, emotional are physical. Another common thing that happens is that a woman takes the safe bet either because she wants guaranteed security whether that security be financial or emotional. Or she's aware that the type of men that she is truly attracted to are not the long term committed relationship type so she shelters herself and either spends a life time being unfulfilled are she uses those men that truly could have her heart for pleasure and entertainment.

For most men, it's hard to allow themselves the opportunity to be vulnerable because after all we are men and being vulnerable is not a role that we have been prepared for, great men have been lost all throughout history by allowing themselves to be vulnerable to the wrong woman such as the story of Sampson and Delihla in the bible. Most men remain guarded and only with a lot of patience and effort do we allow those walls of our on insecurity to be broken down. We are expected to be the protectors, the rock, the pillar of strength. Men are not trained to be emotionally vulnerable. Men that do outwardly express their emotions are often considered to act like females and other derogatory names simply because they do outwardly express their emotions. If you want men to be comfortable showing emotions you have to allow him the choice to be able to pick and choose the things that he wants to be emotional about. You can't be mad if he doesn't have strong emotions about the same things you have strong emotions about. As men the things in a relationship that you feel is important may not necessarily be the same things that we may feel or important. But if you love and honor your man, you should listen and take care of the things that he is trying to tell you, even if at the time you don't quite understand. Most men go through their whole life guarding their feelings and never really connecting on that next level of pure intimacy in relationships where they are comfortable sharing their emotions as well as accepting other emotions as genuine. Some men even go so far as to deal with women that are incapable of connecting with them on a deeper level, that is the reason that gimmick chicks get so much play. Sure they may be cool, fun, are attractive, but they lack what it takes for a real man to take them seriously.

The gimmick chicks are basically those superficial women that may or may not look good but most men find interesting and in a different type of way attractive I say different because the attraction may not be physical and usually not mental but more of the fact that a man is attracted to her freedom and care freeness. The gimmick which is usually a nice booty, cute breast or a certain way she carries Herself is usually what attracts a man to her but these woman rarely have the ability to connect with a real man because their views and perceptions often do not represent something long term and wholesome. Most men prefer these types of women because she can't connect emotionally and mentally he can stay strong because no matter what she does she can't get past a certain level mentally with him therefore leaving him to be more mentally secure knowing that she never had a real shot anyway. It's kind of the same way when women date and marry the safe and secure guy consciously knowing that they gave away their chance at love and happiness and opted instead to go with the sure thing.

Most men spend the majority of their time protecting the emotional security of the woman he loves, sometimes compromising his on in the process by taking deals that may be out of his comfort zone or agreeing to certain understanding that he may ultimately disagree with. As men, we do a lot of work as protecting the women we love emotional stability, we do that by not putting ourselves in situations that are going to constantly require you to trust us. We don't allow situation to get to the point where trust becomes a factor that's what makes the love and the trust grow. Most men want the women in our lives to know that we do love them, but we don't want them to know the extent of our love because the modern woman subconsciously relates a man's love to a weakness and in a fucked-up way it is but it is a good weakness, not a weakness that should be exploited with selfish intentions which is often the case.

If a man is showing you he is clearly not interested in you believe him because no matter what you do he's never going to give you a real shot at a committed relationship with him. He may string you along for his on personal benefit. But all his actions will be used to suit his ownself serving interest. What happens is that women are trained to believe that if they use the P power that the man will eventually come around or they can show that they are ride or die for him while he proceeds to make her look like a dummy. But when somebody was never really interested and doesn't want to be there, there is nothing you can do to make him stay accept for basically give up your soul, dignity and respect and all that is going to do is delay the inevitable.

With most men in general we have a tendency to focus more on the small things then we do the bigger things because as men we expect the big things to be taken care of but those small insignificant things that most women think is nothing is the thing that means the most to us. Most of the time it is the small things that are done that go unnoticed that lets you know how someone feels. Other things that our done may be significant to you but that is just the type of person that they are and not necessarily because you hold a special place in their heart. You must know who you're dealing with before you can decide which because those are the things that are easy to do, but the small acts of service and kindness that are done on a weekly and daily basis often shows you where someone's heart really is even if they have never told you they care once.

FACTS ABOUT CHEATING

Most men are in touch with their significant others emotions and can easily notice patterns in their actions and change of behavior. With that being said as long as we are not too far gone in our on indiscretions we can usually spot when our woman starts to move funny. That does not automatically mean that they are cheating, but it does mean that Something has happened that is causing her to move and act a little different than her normal self. Moving funny is basically when someone is trying to act normal like nothing has changed, but by you being aware and in touch with your lady you can tell something different and significant or insignificant in her mind has

happened. This is also the point when most men began to

wonder about this new found suspicious behavior that is

being displayed. It's usually obvious when a woman has

started to cheat or thinking about cheating or more simply

losing interest in you, all though most women would like

you to believe that there far superior intellect enables them

to go in and out of fidelity whether that fidelity be physical

or emotional and most men would never spot or suspect a

thing. But most of the time we can clearly see a sudden

change in behavior patterns and their interactions with us

men, what most women don't know are don't realize is

that it is the subtle things like different movement

different patterns of speech and overall quality of the

relationship that change. For one she usually starts back

either hanging with old friends or coming up with new

ones, basically finding an excuse to not be around you

more than usual, sisters and friends often make great alibi's

and it usually works out better for them when they pick a

friend or family member that you don't have much interaction with so that no slipping occur, she might attempt to razzle dazzle at this point about how there is no one in the world and how she would NEVER cheat on her man and before she would do that she would be sure to let him know. As men we do usually realize when something is going on and realize the tools and the tricks woman use to make her alibi stronger, her conscious less guilty, and her actions more justifiable.

When she starts being away from home more and start getting the urge to want to do various other activities that don't include you is a clear indication that you are simply not the main thing anymore. Often once the side infidelity gets old or ends she will get back on the team using some lame excuse like she was soul searching or trying to find herself and the best one is that she needed "ME" time. Most men understand the fact that it's not his woman that wants to go "out" it was said friend kept her out late because "you know how she is." A t the time all this is taken place most women believe we have no clue as to what's going on but men that are aware will often give little hints to let his woman know that he is on to her game. The little hints may be something as small as a New-found interest in wanting to discuss your night in detail well as before he would simply ask you if you had a good time. He also might express wanting to spend some time with his lady on a night that she might typically do with her friends or may even suggest that she does same activity only it will be with him instead of them. If a man does this it's not necessarily because he wants to go it's basically a test to see how his lady is going to respond and react to the proposition. But before you put all on the line you have to ask yourself is it worth it. Infidelity is not all about the physical act of cheating but it is more of a mental act based on domination, bias, and selfishness.

For one, if this possible replacement guy was such a good man and so much better than what you have, then why would he spend his time chilling with a woman that already has a man, why wouldn't he just find his own woman. For two, no man really wants to be the backup plan when it comes to woman he cares about. The main reason that men even deal with woman that got somebody is because when a woman already has a man it's fun time and sex without having to be in a real committed relationship where you are expected to provide emotional and sometimes financial support. Too many women that get caught up in the hype, the side dude always seem right because you have the opportunity to leave life's problems behind when you to deal with each other. Most of the time women have a tendency to over hype the things the side dude does such as buy drinks, maybe a gift here and there. Often that's nothing compared to the house benefits, such as rent, lights, gas, health insurance, and the overall satisfaction of realizing that you have a man that is going to hold you down no matter what. The side dude is never going to take you serious anyway because you're sneaking around on somebody that is willing to at least attempt to be in a committed relationship with you and you steady running around sneaking off with someone that has no intentions of taking the relationship to that level that you currently hold with someone else.

Men have been taught to stay away from women that describe themselves as "BAD." Most men don't want a "bad chick" unless it is just a fun one time or weekend thing. A real man wants a woman with strong morals that come from a good family and is emotionally, as well as psychologically, and spiritually stable and has not been ran through by numerous men. Or has lots of MALE "friends," but men do go through the phase where there attracted to the "cute wild chick" because they are experienced, aims to please, knows how and enjoys activities that are normally reserved for men such as drinking and sex. The wild chicks usually make great friends and side chicks but they are not really capable of maintaining a healthy competent relationship that is mutually beneficial for all parties involved. There relationships generally consist of them being taking advantage of, or them taking advantage of someone because their lives have consisted of struggle, pain and games. From the old sugar daddy that they swore they never slept with, to the man that they wanted that was never that into them but constantly pretended like he did to take advantage of her mentally, emotionally, sexually or financially. It's been a life based on abuse so often times the only thing they know to do is to mentally abuse are to be abused. Balance is often not a consistent theme in their life and this is the primary reason for their extreme emotion, lack of focus and irrational behavior. This gives them the power of either dominating are being dominated which in some type of way empowers them (which I don't understand). Crazy is not an attractive quality but many have been taught that this form of behavior is cute and acceptable. Hood Chicks usually always show flashes of potential but I often compare that to a high first round draft pick that never makes it not because they don't have the talent but because they don't have the drive.

Some even marry down simply because although every man's dream is to have a "dime" piece on their arm and be married and live happily ever after that idea is simply not a reality for the average man. We typically find one of two things. We find a good wholesome woman with her morals and values mostly intact, but often times she may not have ideal looks are body type that we prefer but she's solid and dependable so we deal with her. The second type we find is the cute hood chick. Now the cute hood chick upon first glance is clearly a better than the first option because she is fun, attractive, and you have a good time together. (What more can you ask for?) But a lot of the hood chicks are promiscuous because they have gotten accustomed to using men for their own gain and it has been so common throughout their life they often feel the only way that they can get a man to do something for them is by using their sexuality and over friendliness as a way of obtaining their goal. That is one of the main reasons you find so many attractive women in general single, because although it may look nice and be fun most men really choose not to deal with attractive women as their main because it is just too much work. There is no room for error on your part in the relationship and men are constantly on her heels trying to get at her. Most men simply do not want to deal with all that they are with an average chick that fixes up nice. If I want to see highly attractive sexual women I will go to the strip club or the regular club. That's what the club and the strip club is made for, it's a place that you go see attractive women (in theory), although you know 95% are not relationship material they still look nice and all though you might not want to buy the cow, you might like to get a couple cups of milk. Men go to the club to look at and talk to women we know the chances of finding anything quality is slim but we enjoy the sport.

PHONE GAMES

Cell phones have made cheating easier, and if your partner starts acting funny with their phone when you are in the same room, it should be a reasonable assumption that your partner has something to hide. Strange calls at all hours of the night and nervousness every time the phone rings is often a clear indication that something inappropriate is happening and most likely the communication is taking place through their cell phone or other social media apps that they have on their phone. If your partner has a tendency to get hesitant when the phone rings or angles the phone so that you cannot see the screen, it could be a sign that there is something they don't want you to see. Repeatedly letting the phone ring without answering or constantly taking calls in another room are also signs that something that isn't right is going on and their cell phone is the method where the communication is taking place.

Secretive answering in which your partner never reveal any pertinent information about the caller and answers all questions with one word answers such as yes and no should probably indicate that your partner is playing phone games. Avoids revealing any information about the conversation --- often occurs when someone is cheating. When these games start to occur what you should do is analyze the way your partners conversations normally go when they are talking to someone you know, such as a friend, family member or coworker. If you notice a significant increase of secretive language,

you may want to ask what's really going on and confront

the issue head on. When your partner's cell phone starts

blowing up or the text messaging is popping at all hours

of the night, it is normal to wonder who's calling and for

what at such an inappropriate time. If your partner

doesn't have a logical explanation for the calls, such as a

family or a random Facebook status update, your partner

is more than likely hiding something. Be on alert if your

partner starts leaving the ringer on silent, vibrate, or

turning the ringer down so low that it prevents you from

hearing incoming calls and text message alerts. Another

noticeable tactic is when your partner only leaves their

phone in the hands of someone that they trust to not tell

you in case they do get that random text are call from the

person that they are attempting to hide from you. But

when the phone is glued to your partners side and they

handle the phone as if it contains military secrets it's

time to be suspicious. When someone is hiding something on their cell phone, the most obvious reaction is to keep the phone close and guarded from you and your allies. There are numerous different forms of the phone games that people play, but from my experience when your partner isn't moving right 9 times out of 10 it isn't right.

YOU'RE JUST SUPPOSE TO KNOW

I have heard this phrase used often and I have never understood it. Ladies we are not mind readers and I think it is very unfair that you would expect are assume that we know what you are thinking, guessing, or assuming. How are we supposed to know if you never tell us now granted some things are self-explanatory and every now and then we guess right but on average we are going to fell time and time again? I could guess wrong and you look at me like an asshole or I can guess right and look brilliant. Most of the time men are wrong when it comes to what women are thinking because often times it switches from one day to the next and

sometimes hour to hour. So we are not supposed to

know because sometimes you ladies don't know either,

most men would rather be a little cautious when it comes

to ladies and what they want and would rather take the

old school approach of good old fashioned

communication, you know where you tell us what you

want we complain about it and end up doing it anyway

to keep confusion down and because we honestly like to

see the women in our lives happy. You tell us what you

need, want and expect and we do the same. That way

there is no communication break down and everyone is

aware of the others wants and needs. Things don't have

to be complicated and in order for things to be fun and

exciting they must not be complexed and confusing. I

never understood the concept you are not supposed to

just know. You must tell us what you want and expect

first and then if we don't follow through there is a reason

to feel some type of way about that because you made

the issues clear and they still were not follow through.

WANT YOU TO WANT TO DO IT

There are some things that we do for the sake of the women we love and the sake of the relationship. Even if we are together for the next 20 years there will be some things that we don't like and will never want to do. Men are perfectly content if you do something for us that you may not particularly want to do but it is unfair when we do things for women that we don't want to do and you still have an attitude about it. There are a lot of things that we want women to do for us and when they are done we are appreciative and thankful. We feel like baby, I understand that you really didn't want to do what you did for me but you know what I am thankful you did and glad I got a woman that is willing to go that extra mile for me as well as our relationship. I just want to say thank you, where as some women be like, well you did it but you really didn't want to do it you was trying to act like you was having a good time and going through the motions like you really was but you wasn't and that messed up my mood because you did it and all and I thank you for that but you didn't want to. It's not enough that you did it if you didn't really want to. If you didn't want to do it then you shouldn't have done it. But ladies just understand you may never want to watch a game with us and I may never want to go to the nail shop with you but if we do, do it just be thankful that we are willing to go outside our comfort zone to show you how much we are into you.

DIFFERENT POINTS OF COMMUNICATION

I think it should be widely accepted that the point at which a man and woman communicate are different. Say for instance that me and my girl are talking and she says something that I kind of don't believe are disagree with instead of addressing the issue as soon as it comes up I may sit back and think over the conversation and what was said to come up with a better perspective as to how I feel about the situation. This is done for two reasons. The first being to take the time to see if it is even a real issue that is worth addressing knowing that it could easily be turned into a bigger problem and simply turn into a battle that aren't worth fighting. The second reason is to try to figure out if we are using logic are being emotional. When we are at the thinking stage this is usually the point that a woman might start thinking we "acting funny" but that's not the case. When a man thinks he likes to be isolated and alone, when woman think they usually do it out loud and at the same point in which they are talking about it. If men and woman could understand this about each other I think it would eliminate men always saying "she tripping" and woman from saying he "acting funny". If you see your dude a little distant every now and then just let him be most of the time he just trying to figure something out. And real talk if we tripped off everything we could trip off of without thinking about it we would probably come off more emotional than woman. But we don't because we men and somebody need to be able to keep their emotions and feeling in check. So if you think we acting funny give it sometime we'll tell you about it but only after we've thought it out first.

FATHERS VRS DADDYS VRS BABY DADDYS

It's hard for anybody to be a good parent but I think for most men that never had a Father in their life it is even more challenging. In our communities, the family man is oftentimes not the man that is valued and looked upon with admiration it's the dude with all the women the nice cars living the bachelor life. The family man down the street driving a 20 yr. old car so he can raise his kids and save for they college fund is not who we want to be like when we grow up. For most women it's not the dude that come to mind when you thinking

about your future boo thing, boyfriend, or husband.
Most people where raised around or saw fathers in
action but we didn't notice because it wasn't flashy and
consisted of a lot of hard work and sacrifices and wasn't
applauded or boasted about. Sure we all had hoop
dreams, hood dreams or some other scheme that was
going to allow us the opportunity to have the best of
everything but that's not the reality of the situation. The
reality of life is hard and sometime we start at the
bottom do what we need to do and still don't get too far
above that. Although a fathers job doesn't seem
glamorous that's what most men aspire to be, a great
father, not a great daddy and especially not a baby
daddy. I know women sometimes get frustrated with
their children fathers sometime but if he's making any
kind of effort give him credit for that. I look at being a
father as like the PH.D of parenting a very small elite
community and there are not too many examples so it

requires a lot of trial and error. No man starts out a great father but it is something that is developed it's like daddy is the bachelors degree of fatherhood and baby daddy is like a GED.

FATHERHOOD MOVEMENT

The greatest social tragedy in America of the last 30 years has been the collapse of the fatherhood in modern society. Propelled by divorce and pre-marital sex, the percentage of children growing up in a home without fathers nearly tripled between 1960 and the early 1990's. By 1994, 24 million American children where living without their biological fathers (Horn, 1997). Researcher often asserted that children could do just fine without their fathers and that success or failure of a child did not depend on fathers being actively involved in their child's life. The three ideas which led to the collapse of fatherhood were new ideas that were being circulated about parenting, fathers, and children. Beginning in the 1960's gender recognition of both the male and female sex roles gave way to a term called androgyny which basically stated that people freed from traditional sex role behavior would be more adjusted and psychologically healthier (Horn, 1997). Many parenting experts in the 70's and 80's believed that mothers and fathers should raise their children in exactly the same way. The androgyny idea gave way to a new concept called the Nurturing Father ideal, in which a good father was described as sharing equally in all phases of a child's development from the moment of birth. Social scientist had established that most fathers where raising their children wrong. It started to become easier to argue that fathers where not needed in the changing family structure. Some social scientist plainly stated that children don't need their fathers to develop normally. In a 1982 study of fathers – absent households published in the Journal of Marital and Family Therapy, Barbara Cashion claimed that girls growing up without fathers are more independent, having higher IQs, and enjoy

higher self-esteem than girls growing up with fathers.
This according to Cashion is because "two parent family
hierarchical with mother and fathers playing powerful
roles and children playing subordinate roles. In the
female headed household there is no such division.
There is a general lack of conflict, and decisions are
made more easily and quickly" (Horrn, 1997).   the
resilient child ideal was the final idea that contributed to
the decline of fatherhood in America. The idea simply
stated that children are more resilient than we think.
Many professionals believed that children would live a
perfectly healthy normal life even if they went through
major disruptions in the household such as divorce and
other things of that nature. In their 1974 book, The
Courage To Divorce, authors Susan Gettleman and Janet
Markowitz argued that "divorce can liberate children,"
and can lead to "greater insight and freedom as adults in
deciding whether and when to marry and to break away

from the excessive dependency of their biological parents." Similarly, in his 1973 book, Creative Divorce: A new Opportunity for Personal Growth, therapist Mel Krantzler stated that divorce provides "an ambiguous, expanded experience that moves kids to better adjustment in a society that is highly ambiguous and expanded" (Horn, 1997). In the early 80's social scientist began to compile new evidence that challenged previous myths about parenting, fathers, and children. First developmental psychologists discovered that mothers and fathers approach parenting differently, and that these differences tend to be beneficial to a child's development. The new research indicated that the differences between a man and a woman's parenting skills helped to make a child emotional and psychologically well rounded. Research found that physical play with fathers gave children practice in understanding how to regulate their own behavior and help them learn to recognize the emotional cues of others. Dad's style of parenting helped children develop self-control: while moms parenting skills helped children acquire language and communication skills. New research started to be found in support of fathers, for example fatherless children were found to be three times more likely to fail at school, two to three times more likely to experience emotional and behavior problems requiring psychiatric treatment, and three times more likely to commit suicide as adolescents and five times more likely to be poor (Horn, 1997). New research began to show that children where a lot more vulnerable than previously thought and research began to document that divorce and abandonment inflicts severe emotional and behavioral harm. Children no longer where believed to be resilient but often times suffered long-term permanent damage. By the early 90's a new report from the Progressive Policy Institute cited that the most consequential factor in the decline of children's well-being has been the collapse of the American family. The following year, the National Commission on Children released its final report, "Beyond Rhetoric: A New American Agenda for children and Families." Remarkably, the report concluded "there can be little doubt that having both parents living and working together in a stable marriage can shield children from a variety of risk." The Fatherhood Movement is an issue that gained public interest when community based organizations started calling on fathers of low-income families to be more pro-active in their children's lives due to increased violence in urban communities. The fatherhood movement did not reach the national level until the Million Man March October 16th 1995. At that march there was nearly a million people and the focus of the march was for men of all colors and creeds to be more proactive in their communities, as well as their child's lives. As the Rev. Jesse Jackson stated "It's important we have such a march to focus attention on the urban crisis and move from the negative urban policy of chasing welfare mothers, chastising their fathers and locking children up to some real commitment of reindustrialization of urban America."

FIVE THINGS WOMEN SAY WHEN THEY ARE LYING TO THEIR MAN

I just gave him my number so he would leave me alone.

It wasn't nothing like that

That's my play brother

We just cool he never tried nothing.

Why you always think I'm lying.

I JUST GAVE HIM MY NUMBER SO HE WOULD LEAVE YOU ALONE

I've never understood this logic that some women use I have heard it several times but I still don't understand the logic. As a man if a woman I am interested in gives me her number I would assume it's for the purpose of conversation and to gauge each-others interest in each other. A man never gives a woman his number for the purpose of leaving her alone and if I text and you text back I'm really going to assume that you're interested. So woman giving a man your number because you're not interested makes absolutely no sense and it is confusing to us man that assume that if a woman gives us her number she would like for us to use it. Men can be pretty rational and understanding sometime, so if you're not interested let us know so that we can move on. Not be stuck wasting our time on someone that is not even feeling us in the first place. Actually what you really want to say is I met a cool attractive dude that I'm feeling but I'm with you, or interested in you so I didn't give him no play but, every time I see him he be trying to get at me so one day in a moment of weakness because I was mad at you, curious about him, or just lusting I gave him my number with the hopes that he would call. Now I'm pretty sure he has a girlfriend, baby momma, or other hoes so there is a chance that he might not. More than likely it will just be a sex thing so I don't really expect it to take from our relationship and baby here me when I say this I honestly didn't expect to communicate with him this much and I definitely didn't expect for you to find out. But since

you did and I'm kind of caught off guard I JUST GAVE

HIM MY NUMBER SO HE WOULD LEAVE ME

ALONE. Baby you have to believe me I would never

leave you for him. Might cheat though if you make me

mad and I got the right opportunity.

THE POWER OF SHUTTING UP

Often times we are compelled to be right or simply get our point across but sometimes simply learning to shut up is the best weapon to fight negativity and keeps you from trying to understand things that are not meant for your understanding, or it may be that is not the correct time for you to understand. Keeping your mouth closed can be a powerful tool especially in relationships that often turn from a union between two people into a battle of the sexes in which both parties are constantly at war vs. trying to do what is mutually beneficial for both parties. Nagging gets you Nowhere all it does is causes resentment and makes communicating nearly impossible. It seems when it comes to women that most often women nag men about things that we already know and things that we don't know you expect that WE ARE JUST SUPPOSED TO KNOW. If this slight shift in thinking was adjusted the battle of the sexes would for the most part accept for everything else that is wrong that we do. I've found that the key to not arguing is before you both communicate about sensitive subjects grab a glass of water and one drinks why the other talks. It is impossible to drink and talk at the same time there for forcing you to listen vs. reacting like most of us do.

MEN ARE DOGS BECAUSE WOMEN ARE CATS

Yeah its true men are dogs. We are loyal protector willing to do anything for our families and those that we consider close. When you come home it's the dog that wags its tail and is sincerely happy to see you. When we growl that's when you know we aren't playing. We mostly fight over food or the money to get the food. Some dogs fight over female dogs when they in heat but my dogs don't do that. We come in different breeds; you have your full breeds, mutts, poodles, and Pitts. For example, you can't go from a Pitt to a poodle and expect to be satisfied with it. You have to know your pants size when you shop for jeans so it's only right you know what kind of dog is right for you. If you want a housedog it's probably not a good idea to get a Pitt and if you want a dog that's going to protect the house maybe a poodle just won't work. Everybody has there on own lane so playing your part will have a greater impact then being average trying to fill various roles.

Now the cat is a powerful majestic creature and all though you feed it and give it food you never really know where you stand but if the cat wants something you will most surely know what it wants because it will rub up against you and give you the most beautiful purr you have ever heard in your life you making it your goal to please. The cat never needs you it just chooses to allow you to take care of it only occasionally hunting leaving frequently but most certainly always home by dark.

I ONLY HANG WITH DUDES

Personally I don't believe men and women can be friends but on those very rare occasions that true friendship between man and woman can be found. The reason is simple usually the way female and male friendships begin is because one is attracted to the other but doesn't feel that he/she is the others type so they become friends, hoping one day that the other will eventually fall for them the same way that they have falling for that person. On some occasion, the two get so cool that they are no longer sexually attracted to each other, on other occasions sex occurs once and then there are the rare occasions in which to fall madly in love and live happily ever after. On average women that have a lot of male friends basically use the friendships that are strictly platonic to mask the relationships of the "friends with benefits", "homey," "lover," "friend", or "cutty buddy". That way she always has an opt out clause in case her current lover doesn't work out or she's one of those that like to be in a committed relationship, but likes to cheat from time to time. I've actually never met a girl that claims to have all male friends and she has never slept with any of them. Usually it's a couple or more and most times there groupies for certain cliques IE. D-boys, poetry cat, rappers, or real men. Woman are competitive when it comes to the men in their lives so I think ultimately the woman that keep frequent contact with their various male friends is often away for them to hold on to old flings as well as hold them back from ever being able to move forward productively in their current are future relationships. These woman often keep the allure of sex around to keep there "friends" interested. This usually causes them to be labeled a hoe because it is impossible for a woman to contain numerous platonic relationships with men because after all we are hunters and sometimes we hunt when we aren't even hungry.

THE NICE GUY

Is the guy that's nice to everybody and although he does have a lot of woman friends practically all of them see him in this way only as a nice friendly guy not as a protector or providers which leads women to believe that I will not be a great sexual experience. Nobody wants to be the "nice guy." Sure, you want to be known as a nice guy -- but the nice guy? No thanks. The nice guy gets friend-zoned. The nice guy has lots of girls that are friends but not a lot of girlfriends. The nice guy goes through life doing favors for people and getting little in return. Niceness is a wonderful quality. But if it's the characteristic you're most known for, you have a problem. No woman will ever take you seriously unless she has gotten her by her type and want to try something different and even then that often doesn't last long. She will soon figure that a life time of boredom is not worth playing it safe. Or if you're lucky she will keep her nice guy around all the while cheating with the type that she really likes.

FIVE THINGS I LEARNED (I think)

1. You can't be right with other people until you get right with yourself. When you not right with yourself oftentimes you use other people to fill a void in your life that's missing. That's not fair to you or he person that you are basically emotionally robbing because you may need more than what they have to offer and that's not fair to anybody.

2. I learned that if you take care of yourself and do what you need to do everything else falls into place. Sometimes we get caught up trying to handle this and that in other people's lives and neglects our own things.

3. Don't care other people's burdens. If you feel someone has wronged you, let that person know so that, that burden doesn't have to be yours anymore. For years I held burdens against certain people and it wasn't until they knew exactly where we stood was I able to move on. For years, I held myself back because I was letting other people burdens control my actions.

4. Now this one is sad but true, I've learned that you can't expect people to do the right thing. If you think about it that's the reason we have contracts, leases, rules, and rights is because people don't always do what they supposed to do and nobody's perfect so you must always cover your on back.

5. Right is right and wrong is wrong regardless of the situation. Oftentimes we have a tendency to justify our wrongs but regardless of the justification if we do wrong we know it we just try and make ourselves feel

better with words like but and if. Ex. I wouldn't have

done it .

SUCKER BATTLES

Sucker Battles occur because you were either
not up on game, too weak to bring it to the light, or you
just thought it would automatically correct itself. But it
doesn't. Now the problem has gotten out of hand and
you expect the said situation to stop immediately. But
it's not going to because you were initially being a
sucker and let it go on for too long before you decided to
bring it to the attention of the guilty party. What was
once would have been a minor dispute has now raged
out of control because something that could have been
stopped initially without much debate has now been
building steam. Now you're fighting a losing battle

69

because the thought arise to the opposite party, like I have been doing this so why is it a problem now. Even if they know their actions may be a little suspect it still is going to be a battle because you let it to go on for too long. Let's say I being going to the club every week for the last 6 months. I may feel that maybe I have been going out a little too much but my girl isn't, said nothing so I'm going to continue to do it. Now let's say the 7th month she comes to me like you are clubbing too much and you need to stop now. Now I'm automatically on the defensive because this is something I been doing for over 6 months and nothing was said. So even though her intentions may really be about the clubbing, I'm wonder what's the real issue because my actions have remained the same but your thought process is different now therefore making it a sucker battle. If you feel strongly about something you have to express it in the beginning because the longer you wait the less credibility, you get

when you finally express those actions into words.

THE GUYS

Every woman has meet Mr. Funny he's the cool

funny guy that usually tries to be funny and charming

when your man is right there in front of you. He usually

is fairly attractive and witty and your man may or may

not know his intentions. A square dude might think he

cool and funny to therefore indirectly setting you up for

failure. However, watch out the funny guy whole game

is to put you in a scandalous position by manipulating

the situation until he has you in a position of

vulnerability. He may hang around being cool making it

his point to show you that he is everything that your man is not and I don't mean that in a good way. His whole aim is to have you question your relationship thinking about the "what if" with him.

So as a man if I cheat due to a lack of attention and sex why it is that woman cheat for the exact same reasons. How can you be the next man's freak and don't want to give your man that same attention to detail. How can you start off so strong and fall off so quick. Men expect the way we start the relationship to continue just as much as a woman expects us to flatter her with compliments. If a man starts a relationship with a woman even if the basis of the relationship is sex as man we expect that continue. The purpose of starting a relationship is because you both like the direction that the relationship is headed. So that means that that the things that where all ready good and readily available in the beginning should remain available. Feelings are supposed to make love better and take the sex to new levels are so they say, but it sometimes has the opposite affects. The things that you loved about them change and the things that needed a little work are the things that remain unchanged.

If two real people ever have a major Misunderstanding, it's because somebody is not being real as they thought they were, usually its selfishness or some other skewed perspective that causes the individual to have a lack in judgment. Instead of taking the relationship to a fake level, the person that has been offended has chosen to stand on the principles of which the relationship was founded and that's been completely honest about how they feel about the situation that occurred. Relationships don't fail just to fail and most relationship that don't work where over with in the first year but nobody could stand on the principles of their belief system and choose to deal with things internally that they either don't like are care for instead of bringing those issues to the surface where they can be talked about and worked on. Instead animosity builds and hatred develops until it affects the understanding to the point that you start to dislike every movement, word, and action that, that person makes. Trust in a relationship goes deeper than the physical. You can give your body away and to make someone feel certain and maybe fool yourself in the process based on that temporary satisfaction. People give their hearts away all the time but not often they mind.

If you all in with somebody you want to see them on top regardless of if you will benefit from their success are not true friends are not jealous, selfish, are manipulative. You will encounter three different types of friends in life. You will encounter those people that got your back 100% of the time no matter what you do they ride for you and hopefully not have to die for you. Sure, you may have disagreements and fights but ultimately they got your back and when you really need them they are always there. Not saying that they are flunkies are dummies for you but they believe in you as a person regardless of the decisions and wrong and right turns you may make. Those friends are the friends that make you work that much harder to be a little better each day because they are the ones that will make you believe in you when you don't believe in yourself. Those are the friends that will let you know when you wrong and congratulate you when you're right. Those are the true friends that not too many people have. The second type of friend is the friend that hangs around when you are down and out or at least not doing as good as them they want to come around when they have made their desired level of success. When your broke they want to party and hangout, but they never coming about business or ways that you can both be successful together are even

point you in the right direction for you to make it happen

yourself. They are cool people for the most part but they

tend to be selfish and do good things for people to make

themselves feel good and not just for the sake of doing

the right thing. You can't invest too much into these

people because all though there intentions are good they

usually just end up causing you problems in the long

run. The third is the users that only come around when

they need something. I know everybody automatically

thinks I'm talking about money but it's really much

deeper than that. They use you for your emotions, your

spirit, your passions, and energy and once they have

gotten what they needed they disappear until they need

you again. All of these people can be valuable because

of their unique skill sets and the point in your life that

come around. True real friends are what is truly needed,

but you just never know. Sometimes the people that you overlook end up being the most down for you.

Before boys are men we are taught to believe that you respect women treat them right get married and live happily ever after. But early in life you begin to notice that most of the cute girls don't like the good boys. They like the boys that are rough around the edges. Everybody remembers that good boy that got played by the good girl for the bad boy. From that point on boys realized that all though women say they want somebody good they don't want somebody good. Women enjoy a man with a bit of an edge to them. You say you want a great guy that does all the right things but does dudes are boring and unless a woman is fully physiologically healthy she may see a good guy as soft are weak are something to be toyed with. So that has caused a lot of men to harden up and withdraw from the few emotions that we were allowed to show and that causes a lot of

men to become bitter and to really give up on the

concept of a good woman. It comes a point in time

where we stop trying to find and establish something

real to simply playing the game. That's all it basically is

anyway if the relationship doesn't have a solid

foundation and everyone involved intentions are not

pure and honest.

WHO CARES

They say that whoever cares the least about a relationship always has the upper hand. Let's say that you tell your boyfriend/ girlfriend that if I ever catch you cheating We are done. Now let's say that they were caught, but instead of breaking up you talked it out they swore they would never do it again. And even though you went against your first thought you decided to give that person a second chance. Once the second chance was given the battle has been lost because you made a clear direct threat and once that threat was made subconsciously a game of tug a war in sued that caused that person to kind of challenge you to see if you were going to stand on your word. Once forgiven you opened up the door to be physiologically abused, insecure, and having an overall lack of self-esteem. Just because you may be in love and care about somebody doesn't mean that it's meant to be some relationships are toxic. Toxic relationships are deadly like mixing bleach and ammonia it might seem like a good idea but once those core principles in a relationship are broken its best to count your loses and move on. I kind of look at it like a tire you get one flat get it patched up its cool but the patch is only temporary and eventually the tire will need to be replaced. Now let's say the same tire gets another patch. Now all though you still may be able to drive on it the tire that you have is basically worthless and all though you may get a few extra miles on it that patch could come off at any minute. Leaving you a bit insecure and unsure of the tire that you know needs replacing. That's how making threats and not standing on them are in a relationship. It's like that tire that you keep patching up eventually it will need to be replaced.

Walter The Author

WHAT A MAN WANTS

A man wants a woman but not just any woman a man wants a woman that can be a variety of different woman depending on the situation. A man wants his woman to be his best friend. He wants someone that is secure and confident in them and in the relationship. The type of woman that knows when to take the lead but also knows when it's her time to follow. A man wants a woman who is loyal but also doesn't allow herself to be so loyal that she gets taken advantage of by people. A man wants a woman to be emotional stable mentally competent and constantly displaying the ability to bring out the best in people as well as actively working on ways to improve the relationship. A man wants a woman

that makes him feel like a man but also allows him to

treat her like a lady. Someone that commands respect

from both women and men and doesn't allows people to

disrespect her, the relationship, are her morals and

values. And yes values are important most men want a

woman that is a better person than they are. Not saying

that us man are dogs but most men want a woman that is

a little softer, a woman that is a little more gentle and a

woman that is more compassionate and caring than he is.

Maybe a woman that was raised a little better and comes

from a better family and maybe has had to be a little

more responsible. Overall a man want a woman that

compliments as well as helping him develop into the

man that he needs to be for her as well as for himself. A

woman that does not bicker and complain but values

understanding and trying to come up with honest

unbiased solutions to the issues that they may face in the

relationship. A man wants a woman that is confident in her womanhood enjoys being a woman and that wants her man to be the best man that he can be without any of the b.s. that others may face in their relationships, whether it be issues of dishonesty, infidelity, are the various other social issues that affect the average unstable relationship in today's society.

WHAT WE THINK A WOMENWANT

Women are tricky and some women like completely different types of men. Some women like the pretty boys others like the thugs and other like the corporate pimp. Overall, most men believe that a woman wants a solid man. A man that may not have the best job, car, or even looks but always has the ability to make his woman feel like a lady and always is the man. They want a man that is a good guy but not an overly good guy. A woman wants a man that can hold an intelligent conversation and be articulate but can also hold his own in the streets too. Maybe he should have a flaw or two so you won't feel like he's perfect and become insecure. A man that will let you have your woman moments but also knows

when to put his foot down and let his woman know that

he's the man and that some situations and actions are not

open for debate. A man that's semi aggressive, but has

the ability to soften up and cater to his woman when she

needs it or he has messed up to bad (just being honest).

A woman wants a man that has the ability to be able to

take them through the whole range of emotions. You

have to have the ability to be able to make her laugh,

happy, sad, and nervous, excited, and even have the

ability to get on her nerves from time to time.

THE TRUTH

Our past makes us who we are but does not have to define us everybody has experienced some time type of pain are injustice that could have caused us to go down the wrong road. Some have went down the wrong road and made it look glamour's and spectacular. Others have done the same thing and made it look terrible. Some people have made a living off of exploiting others and have had great success, while others have taking that very same path and have had to deal with a life time of pain.

Pain causes people to accomplish great things or suffer a lifetime of misery. The key to pain is knowing how to channel that pain into something constructive and not using it to cause chaos and confusion into others' lives. Everybody experiences pain but most people don't know how to deal with it or handle the pain or handle it in the wrong way. Now I'm not talking about physical pain that's relatively easy to deal with the hard pain is the mental pain that people subject themselves to either intentionally, unintentionally are just due to the result of bad luck and a hard life. But really if you think about it why dwell on things that have already happen or focus on a future that it is unpredictable and can change in the blink of an eye.

I USE TO BELIEVE

I use to believe that the grass was always greener on the other side and that regardless of how you made your money that the only goal was to get rich. I believed that the world was mostly bad and the only people that where not was because they needed to be were because of society and other external factors that where holding them back are they had a belief in God that kept them from there mischievous ways. I believed that there where place I could go and be around people that where so much better than me that I would have no choice but to become a better person. I believed that everybody fell in love and that there was someone for everybody. I believed that everybody else was wrong and that I was right. I believed that when something bad happened it was God punishing us for our sins not even acknowledging the devils tricks and misdeeds. I believed that mental illness was an excuse that people used to hold themselves back. I believed drugs and guns was just a part of life. I believed that the company I kept was not a reflection of me. I believed that every woman that it didn't work out with, it was their entire fault. I believed that I had done enough to be successful. I believed that a couple situations in my life altered the course of who I am today. I believed that my momma didn't raise no fool. I believed that you were only responsible for yourself.

I NOW I BELIEVE

The world cold but the people in your life can make it cool. I believe that for every action there is a reaction. I believe that the company you keep directly affects you. I believe that the devil is out here working harder than most realize. I believe that there are a lot of unreal people in real positions of power. I believe that hard work and doing the right thing insures a better life. I believe that all though there is not someone for everybody if you're fortunate enough to find that one you hold on to it and cherish it. I believe that I don't want to be rich unless I get it the right way and that means not betraying people to get to the top not back stabbing and not taking advantage of people for my own gain. I believe that it's a lot of good in the world but a few make it bad. I believe that I have been a fool. I believe that truth and passion equals success. I realize that I'm not always right and at times I have been very wrong. I believe that I haven't done enough and no matter what point you're in at life you can always do better.

ADDICTION

Everybody is addicted to something which isn't necessarily a bad thing. The only time it is truly bad is when you are addicted to something that isn't good for you. If you're addicted to success, family or loving God then you have a great addiction. But if you are addicted to money, attention, sex or drugs then you are encouraged to find a new addiction.

You want to know why most faithful women are single..? Because hoes are EASY. Having and maintaining a good woman comes with a lot it's like having and maintaining a comfortable lifestyle so to speak. You got to EARN IT. WORK FOR IT. You see,

It doesn't take much to please a hoe... to be with a hoe... to f*ck a hoe... or to control one. You can't just do a REAL woman any old kind of way. That's why all these hoes are TAKEN and a lot of real women are sitting around lonely and getting cheated on when they do think they got something... Because most men don't want a challenge. Not all, but the majority does not. They want what comes easy. You have women out here that make it way too easy for them.

MISTAKES PEOPLE MAKE IN A RELATIONSHIPS

We all know that relationships are tough. They begin with an awkward dating period in which both people are putting on their game face pretending to be the perfect person and the perfect mate. After a few months trust and confidence builds and the mask has started to come off revealing who each other actually are because oftentimes a person acts different from how they believe that they act. People often make a number of relationship slip-ups during these crucial initial phases of the relationship.

1. Giving your partner too much power.

People that give their partner too much power and control in a relationship are headed towards an unfulfilling disastrous relationship. Your partner decides when you go out, who your friends are, when you have sex and mostly any other decision that should at best be a mutual decision. These types of controls are classic examples of one partner believing that they don't deserve to be with a certain type of person, or that they are in no position to make decisions on their own our they are there simply weak minded and can't stand up on there on, some people actually seek out these types of relationships due to there on insecurities and past abandonment issues. A good man deserves a good woman. Tilting the power closer to a 50-50 deal would be more beneficial for all parties involved. A level playing field feels a whole lot better than an 80-20 deal and you can't afford to be on the 20 end of any deal and

the 80 gives you so much control that your partner will
not be respected.

2. Trying to invoke too much of your own control.

Even though it is not recommended that a person
relinquish complete control of their relationship to their
spouse, they should also not be so over bearing that their
actions become controlling. Power struggles can create a
competitive environment, and there is no place for
competition in a relationship unless it's just for fun or
for the benefit of the other party. Truth be told, most
people like some level of control in their lives and this
includes relationships with significant others. You
should definitely try to work within respectable levels
when it comes to control. Whether it's heavy-handed
decision making or a demanding attitude people don't
like being controlled or told what to do. Controlling
tendencies are a sure sign of insecurity and low self-self-

esteem, which eventually leads to hatred and resentment from the spouse that is attempting to be controlled.

3. Over doing it

Pet name and cuddling is cool but sometimes people simply overdo it. Outside of the basic level of respect that you are supposed to have for people, all other respect is earned. Don't be so apologetic (unless you're dead wrong); don't assume that your partner is always right; and don't take the blame for something that isn't your fault. More importantly, don't place your partner on such a high pedestal that they would need a parachute to reach the ground. A truly level-headed person wouldn't want to be that high, and may eventually resent being in a relationship with someone that they could walk or run all over.

4. Complacency.

If you are not exactly where you want to be in your life (financially, academically, or spiritually), it's okay. Most people tend to focus more on the future, so you shouldn't worry about having the world in the palm of your hand when you first meet. Over time, most people will expect to see some progress and eventually some results. Try not to sit idle as life passes you by. Even if you're not the biggest fish in the pond, being tenacious and goal-oriented is all any potential life partner could ask for. If there asking for more, you might want to reconsider who you're with. Because anything that is meaningful will require time.

5. Placing someone (anyone) or something before your partner.

This includes friends, relatives, co-workers, animals, your car, your hobbies, are social media. Now granted there will be times when you would like to hang with friends, or on occasions when you have extra work to do on some new project. Those things should never hold more meaning than your relationship. When your partner feels that someone or something is more important than they are, you may have problems getting them to respond to anything you have to say.

SOLIDER

When you think of a soldier usually the first thing that comes to mind is someone that is strong and powerful unafraid and basically willing to do anything to further whatever agenda it is that they are trying to push. So when you think of a soldier in the ghetto the first thing that usually comes to mind are the cats carrying pistols, hopping out, putting in work (selling dope and other activities that may put them in prison or in a casket) and basically willing to ride are die for his so called block, neighborhood are whatever else is used to separate each other's. But the real soldiers are the men that are either able to shield themselves from the bullshit in the first place or the ones that engaged in the rider lifestyle only to realize that it is all a facade and the things that really do matter are god, family and finances. Sure sometimes we try and justify are actions in the street as a means to take care of or family through the finances that we may receive from those actions. But in reality the streets consume so much of everything that you have in mind and finances you usually end up not mentally or financially strong enough to handle what was supposed to be the point of it all and that's God, family and finances. The real soldiers are the ones that are taking care of their family, doing things the right way, and avoiding the temptations of society and the streets and other so called glamorous yet destructive behaviors. These are the real soldiers. The men going out every day making it happen and often it's with no applause. A real soldier's life is not one of glamour and notoriety.

THE POWER OF THOUGHT

As men we often have a tendency to try and rationalize things based on a logical perspective. While that is not a bad thing the way we think about things have the greatest impact on our perspective than the actual thing we are thinking about. Scandalous people have scandalous perspectives. Weak people have weak perspectives and real people have real perspectives. The type of person you are often determines your outlook on life, your relationships and the situations that you encounter in both. Thoughts get men into a lot of trouble when they act on what they initially think versus examining other possible logical negative and positive perspectives. The severity of the situation also must play a crucial role in the level of effort that you put into the various situations that you encounter. As a man oftentimes we get caught up trying to win every battle that when the key crucial life changing battles come about we are too exhausted mentally to put up a fight.

UNSATIFIED

Many people end up in relationships that do not fulfill them because they enter the relationship with the wrong expectations and for the wrong reasons. A lot of people enter relationships because to them it is a form of completeness. There are a lot of people that are unsatisfied with their lives and their situations and they see a relationship as a way to fill a void that they are missing. Placing the responsibility for their happiness on someone else. Not only is it unrealistic and selfish but it usually results in disappointment in the relationship. Acknowledgement and acceptance to the fact that there is no such thing as the perfect relationship and that there will be issues that will require teamwork and compromise. Most people have the general idea that if a relationship is happy and meant to be, then there won't be any problems and won't require much work in order for that happiness to be maintained but the truth is it's going to be a lot of work maybe the hardest thing you have ever done. At that point, when someone is not willing to work anymore then the relationship is all but over even if the relationship carries over for many more months or in some cases years. If you are interested in finding a person to build a strong romantic relationship with the best thing to do would be to start by focusing on self-first and making sure that your life is together before deciding to share it with someone. Oftentimes people enter relationships with unrealistic expectations are wrong reasons. So once you feel you are in a position.

FRIENDS

It is important to set proper boundaries in your outside relationships for the purpose of protecting your primary relationship from emotional promiscuity. We often think of infidelity as a physical act when the truth is it started as a breach of emotional monogamy. Meaning that most of the time the act of physical intimacy was not how the relationship initially started. Affairs and cheating often occur when couples go outside of their relationship to be fulfilled emotionally when they should be taking that time to develop a deeper relationship with their spouse. Communication is always the key, but sometimes people feel more comfortable communicating with other men and woman outside of their relationship. It is my belief that this is often the reason why men often take cheating and infidelity a lot harder than the average woman takes it. Woman sometimes accept physical infidelity because as men we sometimes go outside of the relationship for strictly physical intimacy. To find women, side chicks that we would never be able to connect with mentally, therefore creating a relationship that could never go past being physical, that in some type of way makes the main woman still feel emotionally secure even if they did find out about the infidelity. Oftentimes men see woman as prey and even though they may be fulfilled in their relationship they may still stray from the house. But woman often seek emotional support from other men when they are faced with some type of adversity are unfulfillment in their relationship therefore causing a deeper emotional connection when the physical intimacy takes place all though they have already cheated both in mind and spirit causing an even greater disconnect from there partner.

COMMITMENT

If you know you're in a truly committed relationship stop entertaining other men especially if they are not clearly a better more compatible option than the man that you are currently with. Now I'm not talking about a bad relationship where both of you already have one foot out the door already. What often happens is both men and women entertain other people that they know realistically they would never be in any kind of committed meaningful relationship with their side piece. With that being the case why even take the time for Therefore now you're boo thing is your main thing leaving you disappointed wanting that old thing back. Now that old thing got him a new thing because you feel for the okey dokey believing you had found a better option. When the truth is that it was just something new and different or old and familiar that was going to eventually wear off and either you the side or both of you lost interest leaving you worse off and either ended a good relationship are made it very rocky. Sometimes in the pursuit of happiness, you end up making yourself miserable for a happiness that couldn't be sustained because happiness starts within and without that you have a need that could never be fulfilled by anyone so you always go looking for more but end up with less. Destroying a long- term good relationship for factors such as convince, excitement, or familiarity that in the end is only temporary.

VICTIM

Oftentimes people both men and women have a tendency to play the victims. If you where the one that cheated in the relationship you are not the victim regardless of what type of justification you give as to why the infidelity occurred. In many situations, the person who may appear to be the victim is actually not and most of the time the cheater and the one who got cheated on victimized each other and on an even deeper level when cheating goes on in the relationship most of the time both parties where either physically or emotionally cheating so the truly honest communication would have been for them to both be swingers and save that false sense of understanding that they shared together. So many times in life we act off impulse not realizing that every action has a reaction. For instance, if you catch your mate cheating but you are doing the same thing or if you get laid off your job but you're always late. Reactions to situations, ultimately falls on you so don't do anything that you're not willing to stand up and be accountable for. As adults, we have to except responsibility for our actions. We all have brains so why not use them! In almost all circumstances their not so innocent.

LEARN HOW TO LOVE

A lot of times in relationships we make the mistake of loving people the way we want to be loved instead of taking the time to learn how to love that person the way they want to be loved. It's a common mistake that people make most of the time. It's because they are not in-tuned with their spouse and other times it's due to a selfish mentality that, that person has to make them believe that there way is the best. So if you truly love the man your with take the time to love him on his level and not just the way you feel it should. Don't get caught up in loving someone just enough so that you get what you want out of the relationship and neglecting his emotional and physical needs. Most men just want to feel like that he is the most important man in her life outside of God

of course.

HE-MOTIONAL

A man that really loves a woman is in an emotional state. I assume it is because when a man only has one woman that he is dealing with he is experiencing a vulnerability that he has never really been exposed to. When a man dates and interacts with several different woman he can never get to emotionally attached to one because when that one acts up he simply shifts his attention to the next woman creating a type of mental checks and balance system in his mind that keeps him from becoming overly emotional about one. When faced with adversity in a truly monogamous relationship for men it is a much deeper set of emotions but when you have a variety of options you don't necessarily weather the storm with the person your with but more so drive around the storm and just wait for it to pass and the focus shifts depending on what current relationship is going the smoothest. So he's never really truly connected just doing enough to get by.

ABOUT THE AUTHOR

Walter The Author writes books, which, considering where you're reading this makes perfect sense. I'm also a military veteran, college educated, as well as skilled in various other trades. Writing, helping others, and motivating others is the real passion. Faith, family, and fun are my 3 favorite F words.

Made in the USA
Monee, IL
05 June 2022